The Sleeper Saga

Geoffrey A. Shelton

Contents

Chapter One: The Cursed Gift

The Sleeper was a timid man
Not popular at all
He just sat in his corner
Just waiting for a call.
He had this strange gift you see
That no one would believe
His words inspire rebellion
Love, trust, and can make you grieve
His life could never be full lived
Due to his cursed gift
For when he got mad his words would hurt
And never would uplift
His poems inspire the weak to strength
Or the proud to take a knee
And he saw his blessed gift
Should be only for glee
He never would unpurse his lips
For fear of what he would cause
For his spoken word could bring Heaven's grace
Or even Hade's claws.
So, the Sleeper was a silent man
Unknown by all the rest
Waiting in his corner
Doing what he deems best.
Dreaming of the better days
Of glory days of old
He sits humming in his corner home
A catchy tune so bold
My small and gentle children
May your lives be so grand

That one day you find love and it finds you
And takes you by the hand
And let the demons fade away
When they hear your gentle voice
By the grace of God they have no power
If only you pray by choice
Never let the pain grow strong
Your father is still here
And when you are not looking
He will whisper in your ear
Use his words of wisdom
Never should you fret
Because the Sleeper man of lore
Has his morals set
Yes, the Sleeper was a silent dad
A man just past the fall
Though not there for most of times.
He loved his children all.

Chapter Two: The Wrath of Words

The sleeper was a silent man
Never outspoken at all
Until the day he saw her cry
Caused by a man so tall.
He stood up in his corner
He thought of what to say
He pursed his lips and opened his mouth
And killed the man that day
He never even touched the jerk
Just told him he was too strong
To hurt the little lady
Then he sang a song:
My fair and charming lady
This man he is not for you
Take this knife with no regret
And you know what to do
The man fell into terror
As his daughter stared and grinned
For he knew in no small part
He had caused his end.
The sleeper was a silent man
Unless he felt compelled
To speak the words of true freedom
For his words were spells.

Chapter Three: Song of Silence

The night was cold and dreary
The moon was full and bright
The goons were out in their full strength
No hero was in sight

The bells rang nine and all went dead
As the melodies began to ring
For behind the chimes all could hear
The Sleeper start to sing

He sang a peaceful lullaby
He sang it proud and true
The goons and bandits- All of them
Had no choice of what to do

First, they dropped their stolen goods
Then they dropped their knife or gun
Then they dropped down to their knees
And waited for the sun.

The police force never will admit
This Sleeper man exists
But our hero is fine with that
For how could they resist

The goons however fear him
Because his mighty voice
Though soft and peaceful in its tone
Takes away their will and choice

His family distrusts him
As his words have power to kill
He goes home to his corner

Speaking sometimes makes him ill

The night is cold and bitter
No goons or bandits out
For just last night their friends were caught
Within his mighty shout

Chapter Four: The Bar Maiden's Lure

The fire was burning briskly
As the tavern maiden starts to sing
Her collection of the favorite songs
That the soldiers often bring
All was quiet in attention
As her beauty drew them in
Another drink for the Sleeper
Sitting on the end
He waited quietly in his chair
Hoping he'd not feel need
To overpower the lady's words
And a new song lead
She sang her sweet lullabies
And she served the soldiers true
She got good tips; There were no fights
He had nothing more to do.
This night he wasn't needed
As he silently smiled inside
"I love your songs my lady
You surely bring them pride"
He stood and walked out to the door
And into the city street
Where he knew the need would be
Evil to defeat

Chapter Five: Mercy of Love

He awakes to the sounds
He normally shuns
"I know that gunfire"
"Twenty-One"
He peers out his window
In time to see them pass
Hundreds of heroes
And flags half-mast
A soldier has died
He's given his life
He overcame fear
And conquered strife
The Sleeper changes his clothes
To a respectful black
He then grabs his pen,
His boots, and his pack
He strolls to the graveyard
To pay his respects
He sees many crying
This he'd expect
But one young lady was calm
Collected, brave and strong
"To cry for my brave husband
He told me would be wrong."
To this our hero smiled inside
And knew her pain so well
Though she puts on a face so brave
Inside she's feeling Hell
He politely took her by the hand
Smiled as if to say

"Your husband will be never gone
If in your heart he stays."
She smiled and whispered in our hero's ear
As she hugged the loving man
"I heard your voice, and you're not wrong.
In my heart he'll stand"
"And remember when you go out tonight
To do the things you do
That even when you're protecting us
He'll be watching over you."

Chapter Six: Surprise or Demise

He hides inside his feelings
But always in clear sight
Yet tonight will test his mettle
For the bullets bring on fright
A stranger has got the best of him
He found and pinned him down
In this lonely dark alley
With no one around
"Give me all your money man!"
The stranger seems so proud
He has outsmarted the silent one
In this alley's shroud
The Sleeper knows he has no chance
To avoid untimely end
If he were to open his mouth
And a lyric send
One last breath before he's gone
Yes, he must fight back
His chance is now or never
To stop this harsh attack
He draws in his breath
Thinks of what to say
To stop this man
Sending him away
When from behind
He gets a shock
One loud bang
From a Glock
"Though at night
You guard our lives

A bar-maiden still keeps
Her forty five"
Sometimes even heroes weep
Like the Sleeper did just then
Not only for his precious life
But she had saved him again

Chapter Seven: The Surprising Truth

The event was somewhat rattling
As he'd seen her face before
He knew her voice all too well
Of this he could be sure
Could this be the woman
The woman that he sees
When he is in slumber land
Yes, his heart agrees
Tonight it seems she saved him
In a much so different way
Than in his dreams when she shows up
And takes his pain away
As he holds his heart to light
His spirits start to sink
He thinks hard, and blurts it out
"May I buy you a drink?"
"Of course you can," his savior sings
Her eyes now filled with glee
"For though it seemed I followed you
I see you were always chasing me"
"I've seen you walk into that pub
And sit and stare for naught
Just waiting for the right words
That maybe you forgot"
The Sleeper is astonished
That she has given him a chance
His mind is filled with happiness
As his heart breaks into dance.
"Tonight the world is mine and hers."
He thinks silently inside

The others must show they're strong
And till morning survive
As they walk up to the Maiden's Mug
Walking hand in hand
He knows he's found his savior
As she has found her man.

Chapter Eight: Silent Voices

"Last night was great. The drinks were good."
Thought our hero with great pride.
Though today would be an experience
With his darker side
"This guy is barely driving."
Scream the voices in his head
"You can make him speed up
Just fill his mind with dread."
When at last the cab has stopped
The driver asks his charge
And much to the Sleeper's shock
The fee is far too large
The ride was only just so far
As to pay a modest bill
But now this slow criminal
Wants his pockets filled
Our hero tells the driver
"Oh this can't be right
Because you see, it was just eight blocks
Without a single light"
"But you see," the man replies
The fare's the same for all.
And believe me mister
The cops won't mind my call"
"Just tell this crook to shove it!"
There's the voice again
"He won't know what hit him
When his mind you're in."
The Sleeper takes a solemn breath
And digs in his pockets deep

"Take this now, and don't forget
The life I let you keep."
As it is approaching quarter till
The Mug's late closing time
Nothing will keep this man down
When his heart does shine
She smiles when she sees him
And he noticed her new blouse
Time to make the drunkards smile
"The drinks are on the house!"
"My name is Cat, my good sir."
She says and winks in spite
Of the fact he never asked
For her sweet name last night
"And I know it's unwise to pry
Into the unknown
But when I ask you for your name
Don't answer with a groan."
The Sleeper takes a mighty breath
As he'd been fearing this for years
He smiles as he has an idea.
"I share my name with beers."

"I knew you were the shy type"
As she draws her roster
Of all the best drinks on the tab
He smiles and points to "Foster's"
"Nice to meet you, my gentle man"
Her smile keeps growing till
His panic is growing far to large
She smiles and calls him "Bill"
Closing time has now come
The customers then go
Now our Cat and shadowsong
Put their hands in tow
Another day and night has passed

Without the Sleeper's aid
But such luck is not long lasting
Soon this debt might be repaid

Chapter Nine: Immortal Memories

On a lonely night in town
Our hero walks in wait
Searching every alley way
Or street to mitigate
He sees the common beggars
He sees the nobles too
He thinks of days of long ago
When he drank the witch's brew
Tonight he simply longs for end
Age will not be his maker
Due to a night of foolishness
His sands are in a shaker
An eternity will pass
And none will know
This Sleeper man of lore
Never older grows
He's taken names from dear old friends
Long after their life has gone
And remembers them in every verse
When he sings his songs
When will his cursed blessing
Of song and verse allow
A nice and timely solution
A way to die endow
Forever living while seeing death
Is no way to live
To live his life and live it well
Was supposed to be a gift
The beautiful enchantress
Had covered his eyes in wool

As you see, she'd been his wife
And he was her greatest fool
Thirteen hundred years have passed
Since that fateful night
Still remembering their anniversary
Cat's alone tonight

Chapter Ten: Reflections of the Past

The night was dark and cold
As he swallowed down his brew
It tasted rather bitter
As glowed faintly of blue
He felt a pain in his guts
And stumbled through the room
At the hands of his wife
He had sealed his doom
Though he felt the hands of death
The potion he then threw
Had he drank the full vial
He'd be dead, it's true
But he saw through her lies
And the false liquid too
So to face eternity just to learn
Was his fate renewed
As he looks back on this day
Thirteen hundred years pass too soon
A natural gift he has earned
As his only boon
His memories are perfect
Of every day, night and noon
Now he is the cunning man
Speaking magic in his gloom
Tonight he is resting at home
But the danger may start soon
"I fear what would happen
If they make my anger boom"

Chapter Eleven: Hard Day of Love

Rainy and cold morning
He woke up in her flat
His mood was confused
As being one so mad
Maybe he had forgotten
Years of pain to hide
For when he is with her
There's an emotional tide
His heartbeat skips wildly
As his mind goes fully blank
And when she speaks, her friendly words
Hit him like a tank
He prepares to go shopping
And she draws up the list
Though last night she suffered wildly
From the touch of love she missed
Our hero was tired but happy
Last night as they lay
In the bed relaxing nude
As his day faded away
Tonight she would not miss out
He'd made up mis mind"
No matter what the cruel world
Does to human kind
He'll take her to the Maiden's Mug
To have a bite to eat
And when they return, his lady friend
Is destined for her treat
Their passion will be amazing
As their hearts speed up as one

Tonight our cunning Sleeper
Will finally have some fun
And tomorrow our lonely hero
Will return to what he does
For the world cannot continue
Without his lady's love

Chapter Twelve: Faith Renewed

Rain it seems
Brings forth gloom
As the Sleeper tonight
Leaves his room
He knows the night is going to be grand
Yet dreads the soggy task
Maybe he'll be lucky
And go to the Mug for a glass
But as he reaches Donner Lane
He knows his night has begun
There is an armed robbery
His songs must be sung
Put your guns down on the ground
You men of hate and spite
Give the man his money back
To it you have no right
Now wait here and recollect
On this night's events
Of how you took advantage
Of a man with no defense
Do you not have family?
You cold heartless swine
Soon the pigs dressed in black and blue
Should book you for your time
He continues toward the Mug in his approach
He's made near halfway
When he sees the mayor
Driving with a sway
He thinks a second of how to act
Then chimes out loud and true

Just because you help make the laws
They are not under you
You are going to get someone killed
Or maybe hit a tree
Pull your Caddy over please
And forfeit your keys
You'll find them in the morning
When you arrive to work
Have a car pick you up in the morning
I know you get that perk
Two songs already in just five blocks
The Sleeper is getting weak
To see his lovely maiden, Cat
Is what he does seek
Two blocks left as he turns on Pine
And his hopes are growing dim
As he sees and hears a battle
Just a few feet from him
I am growing irate and tired
Your kind has got to go
I've been outside in the rain for ten minutes
This you must now know
So, fellows take your fights somewhere else
Or face the Sleeper's wrath
As I have now lost my patience
With all of you riff-raffs
They go inside as he insists
And our hero hits the ground
He must get up and go to her
And let his heart rebound
He fights to open up the door
And then stumbles to his stool
She smiles and takes him by the hand
"Hello my little fool"
As he sits there staring
She gives a little grin

And then to his surprise
He's served blue brew again
"You told me of your curse
And the potion made
And of the effects
Of a lover's shade"
"I did my research to find this one
As you have no doubt
That though you live eternally
You see death as you shout"
"I delved further into alchemy
To perfect and create this brew
And though you barely know me
I want some trust from you"
The Sleeper frowns in sadness
Another Reaper's Kiss
Has now come from his maiden
It has come to this
But as he drinks, to his surprise
He delusions fade away
His energy's returning
He now has the strength to pray
My fair and talented lady
To this I must insist
That this blue drink that I've been served
Be added to my drinking list
"I'm afraid it has quit raining"
She whispers in a voice so dear
And catches him by surprise
As she slaps him on the rear
So out he goes to protect
And do what he must do
But all night he'll wonder
How she purified the brew

Chapter Thirteen: Exhaustion of Heroes

This morning's work seemed endless
As it does more so these days
Tonight, our dear Sleeper
Is working in a blaze
His back is breaking into pieces
His eyes just want to close
As he searches for sinners
He feels his aching toes
Another night of misery
As he is growing numb
To the pains of hard labor
And to his job succumb
People see the Sleeper
As a man who sits around
Waiting for the fights to come
Then his songs will sound
They never really do expect
This hero full of verse
Has not one but two jobs
To make him want to curse
As he sits in his corner
He hears the rumors spread
They wonder if the homeless man
In the corner even has a bed
He stays up all night to walk the streets
Never seen by day
He never says a single word
Must be too proud to pray
But he is never missing
Only overlooked

As during daylight hours
His work has he took
When at last it's two AM
He stumbles to his bed
And finally lays down to rest
And eat his daily bread

Chapter Fourteen: The Nervous Cat

She awakes at ten till one pm
She knows she overslept
There are things to do before she works
Promises to be kept
She rushes for her coffee
And to get her clothes all set
She'll have to dress in her best
"He'll come in tonight, I bet"
She showers and she dresses
Taking care not to trip
Tonight, she'll wear the pink dress
"Oh man, where is my slip?"
She does her online homework
And grabs the secret sack
Of the main ingredient
The Sleeper seems to lack
She must travel safe and calm
Because of the great prize
She just placed in her handbag
Leaves from the tree of life
At half past two she gets to the Mug
And swiftly makes the brew
And places it back in her purse
In case he does come through
Four o'clock and opening time
Still no sign of him
He must be still at work
Or risking life and limb
Will tonight be the night
That she seats him the corner booth

And pours out her heart and soul
And confides to him the truth
Ten thirty-five is when he joins
And she is a nervous wreck
She guides him to their lovely booth
And gently rubs his neck
"There's something bugging in head
That keeping just won't do
I have to tell you something, baby
I hope you know it's true"
Her face drops in embarrassment
As she stares at her shoes
He smiles, and takes her by the hand
"Cat, I love you too"
For all she had practiced
And dressed her best today
He knew before she said a word
Just what she would say

Chapter Fifteen: The Toughest Decision

Time stands still tonight
As our Sleeper walks
Glowing beer in hand
And yet rarely talks
His curse is striking yet again
This is his only fear
The results show it could be cancer
The tumor near her ear
He stumbles and staggers
And most of all he prays
That he'll get to spend more time
With his Cat someday
The evenings are a time of grief
Her strength is wearing thin
Could he slip her some of his drink?
Or would that be a sin
This evening he has just one idea
As he takes her by the hand
"We could be forever here
If you drink my brand"
She shows signs of horror
But also hints of warmth
As she knows the secrets
Of the life-tree's core
"Give me time, my darling
And I'll get a second eye
To look at these grim results
I do not wish to die"
The Sleeper sheds another tear
As he kisses his lady's hand

And says with love and tenderness
"By your side I'll always stand"

Chapter Sixteen: Do Not Resuscitate

He feels a burning as the task is done
He knows he's done his best
To give her deserved longevity
To at least give her future rest
He asked her for a solemn choice
But didn't do so at all
For when she was staring at her shoes
He switched the glasses oh so tall
Soon his Cat will collapse
Into a pain so grand
Hopefully when she awakes
She'll still accept his hand
He knows it was a cruel trick
Based on love and greed
But his lady's tender love
Is the way that he succeeds
The terror strikes him all at once
As she stumbles to the floor
In just a moment her breath stops
And she's seeing heaven's door
"Please stay with me, my darling Cat"
Says the Sleeper as she fades
"If you must die from this
Please let me take your place"
Thirteen hundred years he's waited
He swore he'd never resort to this
But he won't go another day
Without his lover's kiss
She bucks and tosses in her pain
As the potion does its trick

She feels the rising of her soul
But no longer feels sick
"Foster, what have you done?"
Cat then starts to cry
Because now she feels a familiar warmth
Glowing from inside
"A piece of me is now in you"
He says with both shame and pride
We won't live eternally
But at each other's side"
"Now the time has come my friend
To open up your mind to me.
It is the only sure-fire way
To escape insanity"
"Tomorrow you will meet my kids"
He states as he lays her down to bed.
Her reply is quite the shocker
"When will we be to wed?"
The Sleeper is now baffled
How did his lady know?
That now that two souls are one
Together they must grow
Forever in a moment
A thousand years have passed
It seems his lady took it well
And does not feel harassed

Chapter Seventeen: The New Hero

Night-time falls to quickly these days
As the Sleeper needs his rest
He does all that he can do
For the world and his Cat's best
His day-time job brings him trials
His night-time task brings pain
Now he has his love by his side
She will need a name
The Sleeper is already taken
And makes one think of shade
It would be one to describe
Of what she is made
A maiden's name will not suffice
She is more than she seems
She is no longer the tavern girl
Now she shares his dreams
They discuss it through the night
Over cups and streamers
All at once our lady says
"How about the Dreamer?"
So, after dusk the next day
They set out to the streets
And after several near misses
They head home to the sheets
The Sleeper and the Dreamer
They make a perfect pair
Him in his overcoat
Her in his tender care

Chapter Eighteen: Painful Memories

The Sleeper sees the battle
He hears the cannon fire
The lightning flashes wildly
Across the shady spires
This was a time before what's known
A time of myth and lore
He is remembering times of old
But the memories make him sore
He doesn't regret what must be done
He remembers it all so well
This day was one of bloodshed
Before his modern Hell
If at last he survives the day
And gets his duty done
He will go home to his dear wife
And rest in wait for the sun
He takes a rogue arrow to the arm
His bleeding is severe
As he walks in the door
His lover sheds her tears
She gives him a gentle kiss
And makes her witch's brew
He pulls the shrapnel from his flesh
And wrap his wounds true
She serves him up a big glass
And a lie to make him drink
He almost drank down the whole thing
The pain then made him think
He snaps out of his memory
In an ice cold sweat

Now he has done the same for love
He somewhat feels regret

Chapter Nineteen: The Choice of Insanity

He saw the man on the bridge
And he knew it was time
Tonight, both victim and villain
Would be stopped with a rhyme
He was covered in blood
From head to toe
He had reached his wit's end
There was nowhere left to go
He heard his wife was cheating
He'd prove them all wrong
But someone was with her
That did not belong
His rage went unchecked
And he shot them both
He then burned the house
And escaped through the smoke
Now he has nothing left
But his rage and shame
Soon they'll find the body
Of a man with no name
The Sleeper sweeps in
And opens his mouth
To tell the downtrodden
It's not all headed south
"I know what you've been through
And I know what you've done
But you are mistaken
You will see the sun"
The man turns in amazement
As he hears the hero's voice

But tonight, unlike most times
He left the guy a choice
"You can step back from the ledge
And plead your case true
It was dementia, insanity
When you chose what to do"
"She wasn't right
To do what she's done
But trust me young man
You don't need a gun"
"Now is your chance
To start your life new
But turn yourself in
Is what you must do"
The blood covered stranger
Took a step back from the edge
And stared at his listener
Like he was still on the ledge
Then the man simply gasps
As the woman starts to sing
"No one knew it would come to this
When you bought her the ring."
She steps out of the shadows
A woman dressed like she belongs
In a time of long ago
Singing the courts their songs
"Go and do what you must"
She says with no regret
"For when you've paid your penance
Your heart will be reset"
The man breaks out his handy
And dials the men in blue
As our heroes make their exit
As they are known to do
Tonight, was the first time
The Dreamer used her voice

To influence the changing fate
And remove a bad choice
They call an early evening
And head home to the mug
Sipping their fluorescent ale
And smiling oh so smug

Chapter Twenty: The Liar

The night is going fast
Our Cat thinks with a smile
Soon it will be closing time
And we'll walk for a little while
But wherever could he be
He's never been so late
Probably busy fighting crime
He didn't want to wait
Closing time has come and gone
And our hero's still not there
Then the Lovely Cat of his
Hears his voice in the air
"The man we saved just yesterday
Has indeed turned himself in
But that was just the beginning
As we will be next to him"
"He told of what he had done
But then his words turned false
Because you see now he claims
He did so by our calls"
"We are wanted for killing
Not with guns or fire
But by our cursed lyrics
According to the liar"
"I am here inside my cell
Thinking inside my head
Hoping that if we share one soul
You can hear my dread"
"If indeed you are forewarned
Take this time to run

Because when my paperwork was through
Their search for you had begun"
She runs and locks the place up tight
And runs fast to her home
Only to find the men in blue
And they were not alone
The stranger man of yesterday
Was pointing as he screamed
"There's the evil psychopath
She's part of his team"
The heroin is astonished
As to how fast they moved
As they cuffed and frisked her
And into the car she was shoved

Chapter Twenty-One: The Favor

Life is sometimes funny
Tonight was living proof
As she walks in the door
And stands before the booth

The Sleeper stands in uniform
As The dreamer's never seen
Not like the guys in blue
But a soldier dressed in green
She sees the ribbons on his chest
She believes a solemn fate
Is about to befall her
And her humble mate
Then the hero speaks his mind
As his smile grows sincere
"By orders of the general
Our charges have been cleared"
They walk out of the prison
Embraced by each other's hands
"Also the General says hello
To my Catherine, oh so grand"
"He heard about your bravery
And the fact you didn't run
But his only question dear
Was it just for fun"
She smiles as they stroll along
And whispers in his ear
"Two voices are better than one
When you're facing twenty years"
They both begin their laughter
As the Dreamer thinks aloud

"Now that the joke is on the liar
Let's go drink. We are allowed.

Chapter Twenty-Two: The Restless Night

The night was cold and clear
As our heroes walk the streets
Finding more than they bargained for
Plenty of goons to defeat
First one was on Main Street
Robbing people blind
But he was quite the saint
Compared to the knifer on Pine
Cat and Foster take their turns
Repairing people's fates
They engage in small talk
While heading for the city gates
As they approach Park Avenue
They see a mighty fuss
Scattered are maimed bodies
Surrounding a burning bus
"All was well before the boom"
Said the driver with dismay
He knew this was no accident
He passed his checks today
Our heroes help to move the few
That cannot get to their feet
They sing the dying some lullabies
And head home to the sheets

Chapter Twenty-Three: Family Reunions

The Dreamer has a family
And the Sleeper is alone
Thanksgiving has come at last
Cat's offer has been shown
This year he won't be alone
Or crash his children's homes
It raises many questions
Since they are all grown
Though he is their father
He still looks in his prime
While they have aged beyond him
As will their kids with time
Of course his beloved children
Know of their father's curse
But of the eight of them
Seven are perverse
They have all but killed him off
Just to spare the tale
Of their eternal father
Who lives a constant Hell
But one of seven understands
His father's one true pain
And every year on Christmas
Visits once again
This year may be different
As little Adam's sixty-five
And his health is failing
He may not be alive
So the Sleeper pulls his covers down
And prepares himself once more

To another new family
Not knowing what's in store
And Cat and Foster cross the lawn
They hear a laugh so weak
"Thirteen hundred years of walking
Must be murder on your feet"
Adam steps into the light
And gives a simple grin
"I see you caught a cute one, dad"
Then starts to laugh again
"My name is Cat," the Dreamer says
And hugs the Sleeper tight
"My parents will have to wait
Because Thanksgiving's here tonight."

Chapter Twenty-Four: Change of Generations

Tonight will be a special one
As Adam showed his face
He is a month early
Visiting his father's place
Cat cooks up some deviled eggs
Then starts on turkey and pies
Afterward the bean casserole
Which will be the sleeper's prize
"Father, please, we need to speak"
Adam says with a voice so ill
"For it seems that my time is up
And I have no one in my will"
"He would have been your age now
As I'm sure you are aware"
The Sleeper sees the tears falling
And simply starts to stare
"As you have done for years
Now I'll help you do the same
For tomorrow, father, you become my son
When you name is changed"
"Yes, tomorrow, father your name is Lee
Whom I lost years ago
In that horrific accident
But now through you, he'll grow"
"Adam, Adam, can't you see
Your son was so much more than me?"
The Sleeper smiles, and accepts the deed
"In the morning, father, call me Lee"

Chapter Twenty-Five: The Sleeper's Haunting Dream

The night was painted red
As the Sleeper searched the land
For the lady of his life
So he could take her hand
She ran off while he was dizzy
After he drank down the glass
Why had he trusted her
Now he feels like an ass
His anger wreaks his havoc
With every failed attempt
He ends the life of hundreds
Following only his contempt
At last he has found her
But now all love is gone
As he screams and charges
He's awakened by a song
"Your battles are over now
Your pain could be too"
The Dreamer Sings tenderly
Just to bring him through
"Many deaths were born in anger"
The Sleeper whispers in tears
To this the Dreamer smiles
And sings away from his fears.

Chapter Twenty-Six: Mental Flights

The flight was a mere four hours
And our hero was in tears
He was on his way to claim a name
That has been unused for years
Tomorrow he will change his name
Next day on he'll be on the hill
At a local Lawyer's office
Hearing his father's will
Sixty-Five years have passed
Since young Adam's birth
And a short thirty since
His son, Lee, Left this Earth
Tomorrow morning Lee will be reborn
Lost only for a time
When his eternal grandfather
Signs the dotted line
When the flight has ended
The sleeper takes his leave
For there is too much to do
And not much time to grieve

Chapter Twenty-Seven: Birth by Fire

May twenty-second has now come
A day that will not be soon forgot
After signing for his new name
The Sleeper derives a plot
As he walks to find his new home
He plans his own demise
Along with his lady, Cat
To hide behind a name of lies
Soon the family Manor
Will fall into his magic hold
And his lady will fly to him
A tragic story will then be told
"Foster grant died today
When his Apartment burned
Survivors include his grandson, Lee
Who's love was never earned"
When Cat arrives to meet young Lee
She's shocked at what she finds
A limousine is waiting for her
As she leaves her past behind

Chapter Twenty-Eight: The Home for the Gifted

The day is warm and clear
As the Dreamer's arrival is called
When the crimson limousine
Parks outside the mansion's walls
"My fair and charming lady
This home was made for me and you
And in the mailbox was left the keys
And instructions on what to do"
"Welcome to Starlight Reach
She will be a good home
And serve us when we are in need
When we return from Rome"
"Next week we will be married"
The Dreamer says with a grin
As she takes the hand of the Sleeper
And kisses him once again
"But my precious darling, there is more
Adam's gift has a side that's dim
While in daylight hours, all is well
But at night, we use this gem"
The gem is in two pieces
But can be together locked
Just like it's holders' hearts
Whose lives this strange love has rocked
"So place together heart and key
For the whole world's sake
From the son turned father
Welcome to your "Den of Fate"

Chapter Twenty-Nine: Growth of Estate

Standing hand in hand
They lock their key with love
They insert it into the slot
And hear a movement up above
Then they hear a gentle tune
Solemn with no words
The house was changing its purpose
Of this they were sure
They opened the door together
And are amazed at what they see
As this solemn mansion
Was growing much like a tree
Stairs were climbing through the hall
Like roots that need tending
And the chandelier became the stars
Whose expanse is never-ending
As they stroll the bottom floor
True magic is at hand
As the backyard swimming pool
Rises from the sand
At long last they ascend the stairs
And they are in another realm
This place is like a penthouse
They are overwhelmed
Now they see atop the stairs
A key slot split in two
They insert their keys once more
The keys glow a mournful blue
All at once the wall does shift
Like the sands of time

Exposing stars and a flight of stairs
That has a gentle shine
"Welcome to the Den of Fate
You are just in time"
The mansion's roof is speaking
As it's floor begins to shine
Two tables now escape the floor
As from tiles they rise
"Sleeper, Dreamer, Put these on
You'll find they're just your size"
Once the outfits were both on
Their symbols start to glow
The heroes stand on the glowing mass
They know it's time to go
The night was cold and rainy
As the heroes walk the streets
Singing the weak their lullabies
And reviving their lost dreams

Chapter Thirty: The Final Slumber

The night was calm and quiet
But our Sleeper has yet to stir
For years our Dreamer has sung her songs
As she ensures he's not disturbed
His confidence is fading fast
As his end draws near
His hair went from gold to gray
In the last sixty years
His lungs on fire with every wheeze
As he fights each day
To gather up the breath he needs
His final words to say
"My sweet and loving woman"
He thinks inside his head
"I feel the love you have for me
While you are leaning on my bed"
"You think that I'm some hero
That brings the evil to it's knees
But now I must confide in you
I did so with ease"
"Every night of sorrow
I fought for hope to shine
And though I was their hero
You always will be mine."
"And as for our children
You can just tell those three
That though they are just human
They're still stronger than me"
"I have lost a dozen loves
Each time I grew more numb

But my last will and testament
Is finally said and done"
"It seems it's been forever
I've been resting on this slab
And you've been here with me
My wrinkled hands to grab."
"I have been the legend
That crooks and goons do fear
But now my lovely Catherine
I've outlived my proper years"

Our Dreamer smiles and sheds a tear
As she feels familiar call
She kisses her shining hero
And pulls the plugs from the wall
"Thank you Cat. I love you"
Is all he manages to say
She has helped him end his pain
She was his hero today.
So though it may seem shocking
And some people may protest
That what this elderly woman did
Was surely for the best.
Our story ends in bitter smiles
As the Dreamer fades with time
I hope that you enjoyed this month
And of course my rhymes
Love is by far the strongest tool
To fight injustice and the pain
I hope and pray that everyone
Will see the light someday.
As for the "Sleeper Saga"
It had a hidden message to send
That as long as love is in your heart
Your life will never end.

Chapter Thirty-One: The Awakening

The Day was dry and hot
As our hero did awaken
He was certain of his happy fate
But he was mistaken
Every turn on the road of life
Heads toward another bend
And according to his headstone
He was born on the tenth
"This is not right, it cannot be."
Lee Grant said aloud
"For when I was born on the thirteenth
It drew quite the crowd"
Our hero was an observant man
Who often took a glimpse
Into new realities
Which made him oh so tense
In his Casket, he finds a clue
A single tattered letter
"Your family awaits you dear
Return when you are better"
He knows the signature all too well
It takes him by surprise
It was written in his mother's hand
He can't believe his eyes
He finds his clothes beside the bed
As his imagination fades
He had thought he was in a coffin
Covered only in shades
But now his eyes are opened
And now he truly sees

That the last fourteen hundred years
Was just a fantasy
He places on his sneakers
And grabs his backpack up
And on his way out the front door
He feeds the family pup
"I know when they see me
It will stir a lot of grins"
He looks at the itinerary
Scheduled for the tenth.

Chapter Thirty-Two: The Eternal Choice

He received the call
Just after five
She was badly hurt
But still alive
Her husband fell
And his true form showed
Now he took all her things
Into his abode
He cast her aside
And broke his word
She trusted him
Which was absurd
The Sleeper woke in pain
His last path was shown
He had to at long last
Take his place on the throne
The lonely traveler
Cried his tears
As he looked back fondly
Through his years
His father by love
But not by blood
Had foolishly sunk
To throwing mud
Now the unfortunate father
Meets his deserved fate
As the Sleeper takes
His mother's mate
With a flash of silver light
From within the Sleeper

All is forgotten to time
As born is the Reaper
The man is struck breathless
As his world is dimming
And he is struck with horror
As the Reaper starts grinning
"Don't beg for your life"
Our crazed hero sings
"For you know it is useless"
He then sprouts his wings
Angel of Death to some
Hero to some others
The world will soon know
That this man smothered
He gave his word
And it was covered in lies
He forced a hero's wrath
To finally rise
With a single word
The Reaper's curse was broke
As his father fell silent
When commanded to "Choke"
Karma is reality
And his pain was real
As the Reaper smiled
And the man's fate was sealed
His life was gone
As was a hero's soul
Even an angel's good deed
Still takes its toll

Chapter Thirty-Three: The Final Secret

Class was long and boring
As Foster starts to blink
The instructor does not notice
As the young man starts to sink
Sinking into madness
Falling into dream
He leaves this world behind him
As his eyes begin to gleam
He sees the knights of old
He sees the maidens fair
Then he feels the growing
Of his long golden hair
Once again the Sleeper reigns
As the villains fall in pain
Because you see the Sleeper
Is singing once again
The teacher tries to wake him
But his efforts are to no avail
As our hero had one last secret
That now he must share
He has suffered a tumor in his brain
That was his greatest tool
And now inside his greatest dream
Forever he will rule
His parents are torn apart in sorrow
Until they see his smile
For now they know that their son
Is walking along the Nile
He had dreamed for many years
Of traveling this world

The only thing he was waiting for
Was his favorite girl.
When at last his room is set
At the hospital in town
Mom and Dad find the lady
By his bed dressed in a gown
Though he never got his dance
They see he has no pain
And the fair and charming lady
Is beside his bed again
"Dear Foster, this kiss is yours
For everything you are"
The lady gently leans in
And takes him by the arm
"When in the morning, your son wakes
Tell him the Dreamer came to see
Just what it is the Sleeper has not told.
His darling Cat was me"

Epilogue of The Sleeper Saga

I hope you liked this story
As his journey you did learn
That as our hero Foster lived
For good his heart did yearn
May your days or years be merry
May you never grieve and cry
For in every poem is a prayer.
You can find inside.
May you always read and smile
As the stories flood the page
As the joyous saga unravels
To each and every age.

Made in the USA
Monee, IL
20 December 2020

54688743R00036